This edition published by Ravette Publishing 2006.

Printed and bound in Belgium

ISBN 10: 1-84161-256-1
ISBN 13: 978-1-84161-256-0

ℛℛ
RAVETTE PUBLISHING

Lead me not into temptation, I can find the way myself

I eat all the
main food groups,
microwave,
fast and
frozen

I'd give up cake, but I'm no quitter

Fridge pickers
wear
bigger
knickers

I'm on a
Gin and Tonic diet,
so far I've lost
two days

Save the Earth,
it's the only
planet with
chocolate

Never eat
more
than you can
lift

At Easter
size
does count

I keep trying
to lose weight,
but it keeps
finding me

If they don't have cake in heaven I'm not going!

Lord if you won't make me skinny, please make my friends fat

There's nothing better than a good friend except a good friend with chocolate

I love to
cook with wine,
sometimes
I even put it in
the food

So much

chocolate log,

so little time

I take life with a pinch of salt, a wedge of lime and a shot of tequila

Man cannot
live by cake
alone, but
woman
can

A balanced diet is a burger in each hand

Other BORN TO SHOP titles available ...

	ISBN	Price
Another day in paradise	1 84161 255 3	£4.99
Friends are the family we choose for ourselves	1 84161 254 5	£4.99
All men are created equal ... equally useless	1 84161 257 X	£4.99

HOW TO ORDER   Please send a cheque/postal order in £ sterling, made payable to 'Ravette Publishing' for the cover price of the books and allow the following for post & packaging ...

UK & BFPO	70p for the first book & 40p per book thereafter
Europe & Eire	£1.30 for the first book & 70p per book thereafter
Rest of the world	£2.20 for the first book & £1.10 per book thereafter

RAVETTE PUBLISHING LTD
Unit 3 Tristar Centre
Star Road
Partridge Green
West Sussex RH13 8RA
Tel: 01403 711443 Fax: 01403 711554 Email: ravettepub@aol.com

Prices and availability are subject to change without prior notice.